READING JESUS' PARABLES
WITH DAO DE JING

Reading Jesus' Parables with Dao De Jing

Appendix: A New Translation of the Dao De Jing

Yung Suk Kim

RESOURCE *Publications* • Eugene, Oregon

READING JESUS' PARABLES WITH DAO DE JING
Appendix: A New Translation of the Dao De Jing

Copyright © 2018 Yung Suk Kim. All rights reserved. Except for brief quotations in critical publications or reviews, no part of this book may be reproduced in any manner without prior written permission from the publisher. Write: Permissions, Wipf and Stock Publishers, 199 W. 8th Ave., Suite 3, Eugene, OR 97401.

Resource Publications
An Imprint of Wipf and Stock Publishers
199 W. 8th Ave., Suite 3
Eugene, OR 97401

www.wipfandstock.com

PAPERBACK ISBN: 978-1-5326-5491-6
HARDCOVER ISBN: 978-1-5326-5492-3
EBOOK ISBN: 978-1-5326-5493-0

Manufactured in the U.S.A.   05/21/18

Contents

Preface | vii

1 Introduction | 1
2 Parables from the Perspective of "Impartiality" | 5
3 Parables from the Perspective of "Smallness" | 10
4 Parables from the Perspective of "Softness/Weakness" | 15
5 Parables from the Perspective of "Gravity" | 20
6 Parables from the Perspective of "Lowliness" | 24
7 Conclusion | 28
Appendix: A New Translation of the Dao De Jing | 31

Resources for Further Study | 65

Preface

Dao De Jing is an ancient wisdom book, purportedly written by Laozi, who flourished in the sixth century BCE according to the Chinese tradition. It comprises of eighty-one short poems of which the source is diverse, ranging from personal life to communal and political life. It uses abundant metaphors taken from nature such as water, dust, river, wood, river, and valley. Laozi reminds his readers to rethink their worldview and purpose of life. Parables of Jesus also are stories about life, ranging from personal identity to social justice. Laozi and Jesus lived in different places at different times. Yet they share a passion and vision to make a better world, full of mercy, justice, and peace. Laozi asks his audience to appreciate the power of smallness in their perspectives. Likewise, in the Mustard Seed, Jesus also helps his audience to see the potential of small seed that may grow miraculously to several feet tall. This book reads Jesus' parables from the perspective of the Dao De Jing. There is a new translation of the Dao De Jing in the Appendix.

1

Introduction

Dao De Jing is a world-classic wisdom book and offers an alternative way of life that is rooted in nature. It seeks to deconstruct the conventional wisdom, and its paradoxical language is compared to the parables of Jesus. It is very critical of systemic evil as well as personal ills. It asks fundamental life-related questions such as: What is an ideal life? What can we do as we seek an ideal life? In some way, Dao De Jing is close to Jacques Derrida's critique of logocentrism and seeks to deconstruct the dominant ideology of powers and prerogatives of elites. It also criticizes all political greed and asks humans to return to the basics of life, which is a humbling spirit and simple life. People should be like water or dust. When they follow the way of nature, their thought, behavior, and attitude will cohere with it. All who live according to that rule would be virtuous. Therefore, the Dao ("Way") is inseparable from De ("Virtue").

Reading Jesus' Parables with Dao De Jing

Key Perspectives of the Dao De Jing

Wisdom/Enlightenment

- Zì zhī zhě míng: "Those who know themselves are enlightened" (Dao De Jing 33). Those who know others are called clever, but those who know themselves are wise or enlightened.
- Jiàn xiǎo yuē míng: "To see small is enlightenment" (52). Often we do not see great potential in smallness. All beginnings are small. "The tallest tree begins as a tiny sprout. A nine-story tower begins with one shovel of dirt. A journey of a thousand miles starts with a single step" (64).
- Tóng qí chén: "Become with the dust" (4, 56). "Dust" is a metaphor or metonymy that represents small thing. They must know they are small.
- Fǎn zhě dào zhī dòng: "To return is the movement of the Way" (40). To what people must return? It is the sense of smallness or dust. Interestingly, the idea of "to return" echoes the Hebrew verb *shub* ("to turn back") and the Greek verb *metanoeo* ("to change a mind").

Strength

- Zì shèng zhě jiàng: "The wise conquer themselves and therefore they are strong" (33). Those who conquer others are forceful, but those who conquer themselves are strong. These people are supposed to be like weak or soft like water.
- Shǒu róu yuē jiàng: "To keep softness is strength" (52). In the Dao De Jing, the ideal way of life is to be like water, which is soft (chapter 3–4, 10, 36, 43, 52, 55–56, 58, 76, 78) and weak (chapter 29, 36, 55, 76, 78). A virtuous person is like a newborn infant whose bones are soft, muscles are weak, and yet their grip is secure.

Introduction

- Shǎng shàn ruò shuǐ: "Water is the best thing in the world" (8). Water does not compete with things in the world; rather, it flows to lower places such as rivers and seas. Simply, water is humble and serves all.

- Ruò zhě dào zhī yòng: "To be soft or weak is the function of the Way" (40). Water is soft or weak, and therefore it is very useful. If water is hard, it is useless. This idea may apply to the human world.

Impartiality

- Tiān dì bù rén: "Heaven and earth are impartial" (5). Heaven is vast and empty; it does not seek its own will but does great works for all. Like a bellows, what is empty inside can produce more than what is filled with.

Reversal

- Dà zhí ruò qū: "What is most straight seems devious" (45). Dao De Jing 77 has also a similar saying: "The Way of heaven reduces what is excessive and supplements what is insufficient. The humanistic way is different. It reduces the insufficient and increases the excessive."

Dao De Jing and Bible

Interestingly, both the Dao De Jing and the Bible were written around the sixth century BCE, which is the time of intellectual revolution in the East and West. All books in the Hebrew Bible (*TaNaKh*, which stands for Torah, Nevi'im, and Ketuvim, respectively) contain Jewish wisdom and history, shaped by their historical, religious experience. Dao De Jing is a short book composed of eighty-one poems. Obviously, it is not a religious book. The origin and context of the two traditions (Dao De Jing and the Bible) are certainly very different. Nevertheless, they have some in common. Dao De Jing teaches that we are very limited and should seek the way of nature; for example: "Become one with dust; to see small is enlightenment; to keep softness is strength." Biblical traditions also teach this same point. For example, God's way is beyond the human way (Isaiah 55:1–9). Paul also considers "weakness" as a virtue: "I am strong when I am weak" (2 Corinthians 12:10).

Dao De Jing and the Parables

Dao De Jing is composed of a variety of poems of which the source is diverse, ranging from personal life to communal and political life. It is much like parable in the way that it helps readers to see something differently. Parable comes from the Greek *parabole*, which means "to be cast alongside."[1] So it is "a story cast alongside of life for the sake of leading the audience to see something differently."[2] Dodd's definition of parable is also helpful: "At its simplest the parable is a metaphor or simile drawn from nature or common life, arresting the hearer by its vividness or strangeness, and leaving the mind in sufficient doubt about its precise application to tease it into active thought."[3] We will read Jesus' parables from the perspectives of the Dao De Jing.[4]

---

1. See Gowler, *What Are They Saying about the Parables?*, 42–43.
2. Borg, *Jesus*, 259.
3. Dodd, *The Parables of the Kingdom*, 5.
4. Parable interpretation in this book derives from my early publication: *Jesus's Truth: Life in Parables*.

2

Parables from the Perspective of "Impartiality"

Dao De Jing 5

Heaven and earth are impartial. They treat all things as straw dogs. The wise are also impartial. They treat people as straw dogs. Heaven and earth are like a bellows. While empty, it is never exhausted. The more it is worked, the more it produces. Much talk counts little. Keep focused on the inside of you.

Dao De Jing 7

Heaven and earth are big, lasting long because they do not live for themselves. The wise put themselves behind; therefore, they advance. Giving up themselves, they find themselves. Giving up selfish desire, they fulfill themselves.

The central theme of Dao De Jing 5 is "Heaven and earth are impartial to all" (tiān dì bù rén). Heaven is impartial and treats

Reading Jesus' Parables with Dao De Jing

all the same. Nobody can avoid natural disasters. The sun and the moon shine upon all. The wind blows to all, big and small houses, plazas and streets. It favors nothing. Earth is also impartial. The conditions of the earth are the same with all. Heaven is vast and empty. It does not seek its own will but does great works for all. Like a bellows, what is empty inside can produce more than what is filled with. "Heaven and earth are lasting long" (tiān cháng dì jiǔ) because they do not seek their own desires (Dao De Jing 7).

Sower (Mark 4:3b-8; see also Matt 13:3-9; Luke 8:5-8; Thomas 9)

> 3 Listen! A sower went out to sow. 4 And as he sowed, some seed fell on the path, and the birds came and ate it up. 5 Other seed fell on rocky ground, where it did not have much soil, and it sprang up quickly, since it had no depth of soil. 6 And when the sun rose, it was scorched; and since it had no root, it withered away. 7 Other seed fell among thorns, and the thorns grew up and choked it, and it yielded no grain. 8 Other seed fell into good soil and brought forth grain, growing up and increasing and yielding thirty and sixty and a hundredfold.

In the Parable of the Sower, "the reign of God" (*basileia theou*)[1] is compared to a sower who "went out to sow." If he has a certain wider area that he has to sow, he must scatter seeds so that they may fall on such a wider area. He does not decide on which parts of the land he will sow. He takes a risk of losing or wasting some seeds because he knows some may fall on unintended places such as the path, the rocky ground, and among the thorns. But he does not care about that because his focus is on the entire land. Even if he loses or wastes seeds, he thinks it is a necessary cost that cannot be compared with the abundant harvest. He scatters seeds and tries to cover a wider area. But this is not the end of his work; he will plow the land after sowing, which is a general practice of

---

1. *Basileia theou* means God's reign or his activity. It is not a place.

Parables from the Perspective of "Impartiality"

farming in those days.[2] Since he will plow later, he can sow seeds with confidence.

Seed Growing Secretly (Mark 4:26–29)

> 26 The kingdom of God is as if someone would scatter seed on the ground, 27 and would sleep and rise night and day, and the seed would sprout and grow, he does not know how. 28 The earth produces of itself, first the stalk, then the head, then the full grain in the head. 29 But when the grain is ripe, at once he goes in with his sickle, because the harvest has come.

In the Parable of the Seed Growing Secretly, the reign of God is compared with someone who would scatter seed on the ground. But his job is very limited. There are not many things he can do. The only thing he must do is scatter seed on the ground. Otherwise, many good necessary conditions are given to him: good seeds, proper weather and season, and the ground. He does not make good seeds that have life within it. Weather and seasons are also given and necessary to the growth of the seed. All these things are useless without the ground to which the seed is sown. The ground is impartial and it takes whatever is sown and produces the proper grain or fruit. In this parable, what is impartial is not the sower but the ground and other conditions given. Once the seed is sown, it would sprout and grow. In a sense, life begins and grows without humans, whose job is to sow seed and to wait until the harvest.

Vineyard Workers (Matthew 20:1–16)

> 1 For the kingdom of heaven is like a landowner who went out early in the morning to hire laborers for his

---

2. This sower resembles the character of God that Jesus emphasizes in Matt 5:45: "But I say to you, Love your enemies and pray for those who persecute you, that you may be children of your Father in heaven; for he makes his sun rise on the evil and on the good, and sends rain on the righteous and on the unrighteous."

Reading Jesus' Parables with Dao De Jing

vineyard. 2 After agreeing with the laborers for the usual daily wage, he sent them into his vineyard. 3 When he went out about nine o'clock, he saw others standing idle in the marketplace; 4 and he said to them, 'You also go into the vineyard, and I will pay you what is right or just.' So they went. 5 When he went out again about noon and about three o'clock, he did the same. 6 And about five o'clock he went out and found others standing around; and he said to them, 'Why are you standing here idle all day?' 7 They said to him, 'Because no one has hired us.' He said to them, 'You also go into the vineyard.' 8 When evening came, the owner of the vineyard said to his manager, 'Call the laborers and give them their pay, beginning with the last and then going to the first.' 9 When those hired about five o'clock came, each of them received the usual daily wage. 10 Now when the first came, they thought they would receive more; but each of them also received the usual daily wage. 11 And when they received it, they grumbled against the landowner, 12 saying, 'These last worked only one hour, and you have made them equal to us who have borne the burden of the day and the scorching heat.' 13 But he replied to one of them, 'Friend, I am doing you no wrong; did you not agree with me for the usual daily wage? 14 Take what belongs to you and go; I choose to give to this last the same as I give to you. 15 Am I not allowed to do what I choose with what belongs to me? Or are you envious because I am generous (*agathos: good*)?' 16 So the last will be first, and the first will be last.

In the Parable of the Vineyard Workers, the landowner's perspective is very different from typical masters in society. He has an impartial perspective toward all workers in his vineyard regardless of what time they joined his vineyard. He thinks all workers need equal pay to support their family. In other words, his simple perspective is justice for all. This kind of justice is called "distributive justice."[3] In normal society, people can be paid well, based on working hours. This dictum may work: "The more work you do,

---

3. The landowner's perspective may be understood better through "dà zhí ruò qū" in Dao De Jing 45: "What is most straight seems devious."

Parables from the Perspective of "Impartiality"

the more you will be paid." This is what we call "attributive justice." But in some situation, this justice will not work because there are some weak or sick people who are not able to compete with other "strong" people. It is possible that some came to the marketplace late because of those hampering conditions. But the landowner hires all of them by going out to the marketplace five times from early morning to late afternoon, which is very unusual. More than that, he promises to pay "what is just" (or "the usual daily wage"), which is also unusual. Now when the pay time comes, all received the same. Those who came early to the vineyard complained to the landowner because they thought they would receive more. But in fact, they do not need more than what they receive. They become envious or greedy when they see others to be paid the usual daily wage. In fact, they agreed to work with the usual daily wage. They need a simple, impartial mind that others also need a good pay.

3

Parables from the Perspective of "Smallness"

Dao De Jing 52

All things in the world have a beginning, which is called the great mother. Once we have found the mother, thereby we understand the child. Once we know the child, we return to keep the mother. Abiding by the mother, we are free from danger even when the body may die. Curve your tongue and senses. You will not be worn out until you die. If you open your senses with a busier mind and busier activities, you will remain helpless in your life. To see small is enlightenment. To keep softness is the strength. Use the light and return to enlightenment without harming others. This is the way of practicing the eternal.

Dao De Jing 64

Things are easier to control while they are quiet. Things are easier to plan before they manifest omens. Things

Parables from the Perspective of "Smallness"

break easier while they are still frail. Things are easier to scatter while they are still small. Prevent problems before they arise. Take action before things get too difficult. The tallest tree begins as a tiny sprout. A nine-story tower begins with one shovel of dirt. A journey of a thousand miles starts with a single step. If you interfere with things and rush into them, you will fail. If you hold on to things, you will lose them. The wise do not fail because they do not interfere, leaving things to take their course. The wise do not lose things because they do not hold on to them. People usually fail when they are about to succeed. Be as careful of the end by the beginning, and there will be no failure. Therefore, the wise desire no desire. They do not value rare treasures. They learn to unlearn and return to what many have missed so all things may be natural without interference.

The wise people know that they are small.[1] In Dao De Jing 52, Jiàn xiǎo yuē míng means "to see small is enlightenment." In other words, they must identify with the dust, as we have a similar phrase in Dao De Jing 56: tóng qí chén ("Become one with the dust"). When they know they are small, they would be enlightened. This idea is also expressed in Dao De Jing 33: "Those who know themselves are enlightened" (zì zhī zhě míng). We always must return to this idea of smallness: fǎn zhě dào zhī dòng ("to return is the movement of the Dao," 40). Similarly, we have the following in Dao De Jing 64: "The tallest tree begins as a tiny sprout. A nine-story tower begins with one shovel of dirt. A journey of a thousand miles starts with a single step."

---

1. Dao De Jing 63 has the following that emphasizes the importance of "small" in a different way: "Regard the small as great. Regard the few as many. Repay enmity with virtue. Deal with the difficult while it is still easy. Begin great works while they are still small. Difficult tasks begin with what seems easy, and great accomplishments begin with what is small. Because the wise try nothing too big, they can accomplish big things. Those who make easy promises lack faithfulness. Those who think everything is easy will encounter many difficulties. The wise always confront difficulties and therefore have no difficulty."

Reading Jesus' Parables with Dao De Jing

Mustard Seed (Mark 4:30-32; see also Matt 13:31-32; Luke 13:18-19; Thomas 20)

> 30 He also said, "With what can we compare the kingdom of God, or what parable will we use for it? 31 It is like a mustard seed, which, when sown upon the ground, is the smallest of all the seeds on earth; 32 yet when it is sown it grows up and becomes the greatest of all shrubs, and puts forth large branches, so that the birds of the air can make nests in its shade."

While Luke does not describe the size of the mustard seed, Mark says it is "the smallest of all the seeds on earth." Matthew also says it is "the smallest of all the seeds." But in reality, the mustard seed is not the smallest seed on earth or the smallest seed of all the seeds. The issue is not whether the mustard seed is the smallest. This parable is not about horticulture or science. The other issue is whether this mustard plant becomes a tree. In Mark, the mustard seed "becomes the greatest of all shrubs, and puts forth large branches . . . so that the birds of the air can make nests in its shade." The branches of the mustard plants are strong enough, and its shade is good enough for the birds of the air. But Matthew and Luke say the mustard seed becomes a tree. But in reality, the mustard plant is not a tree. But it is like a tree, functioning as a tree, benefiting others.

We wonder why Jesus does not say that the reign of God is like a cedar tree, which is gorgeous and tall.[2] Jesus surprises his audience by telling them that God's reign is like a mustard seed. People think the mustard seed is too small to be great. But it becomes a tree on which the birds of the air can make nests. The height of a tree is not important for the birds. A small tree also makes shades and shelters for the needy. Though the mustard tree

---

2. A cedar tree is the king of the trees, growing on the high snowy mountains in Lebanon, 2000 meters from the sea level; its height is 40m high; its diameter of 3m, and lifespan of 2-3000 years. The cedar tree appears 70 times in the OT; it is a deluxe wood material used for palaces (Ps 104:16). Cedar represents glory (Isa 35:2; 60:13), power (Ps 29:5), magnificence (1 Kgs 19:23; Isa 2:13), and authority (1 Kgs 4:33; 2 Kgs 14:9; Zech 11:1).

or plant grows about several feet high, living only a few years, it grows big enough to serve the birds of the air. It can be also used for food or medicine. It is everywhere and spreads like wildfires. From a different perspective, it is beautiful and useful. Small seed has great potential.

Leaven (Matt 13:33; see also Luke 13:20-21)

> He told them another parable: "The kingdom of heaven is like yeast that a woman took and mixed in with three measures of flour until all of it was leavened."

In the Parable of the Leaven we also see a similar theme of smallness. A small portion of leaven is needed to making bread big and tasty. But leaven would be useless unless it were placed in the right place. Thus in this parable, a woman "took and mixed in with three measures of flour until all of it was leavened." She recognizes the power of small leaven and mixes it with flour. Leaven must be mixed with a large amount of flour until all of it was leavened. The implication is that in God's rule, small thing, small gift, or small person can be very effective once it is used in the right place.

Lost Sheep (Matt 18:12-14; see also Luke 15:3-7)

> 12 What do you think? If a shepherd has a hundred sheep, and one of them has gone astray, does he not leave the ninety-nine on the mountains and go in search of the one that went astray? 13 And if he finds it, truly I tell you, he rejoices over it more than over the ninety-nine that never went astray. 14 So it is not the will of your Father in heaven that one of these little ones should be lost.

A shepherd has a hundred sheep. If one of them is lost, he will search for the lost one, leaving the nine-nine on the mountains. But this is a hard job. Sometimes or most times the shepherd may not know when such a loss happens. If the shepherd does not have a simple mind that cares for all, without favoritism, he/she would

Reading Jesus' Parables with Dao De Jing

not be aware of such a loss. The good shepherd must keep attention to all of his sheep because they are precious. If one is lost, it also is precious and cannot be given up. He does everything he can to find it. One sheep is not insignificant because it is also precious.

4

Parables from the Perspective of "Softness/Weakness"

Dao De Jing 8

Water is the best thing in the world. It benefits all things without competing with them. It flows to lower places that people do not want to go. Therefore it is closest to the Way. Look for lowly places. Look into the depth of all things. Treat others with mercy. Speak trusting words. Do right things when governing. Act mercifully and timely. Do not compete with others and there will be no fault with you.

Dao De Jing 40

Reversion is the movement of the Way. Weakness is the function of the Way. All things in the world come from being. Being comes from non-being.

Water flows into the lowly places, benefitting all. It does not fight to get more. It does not have splendid colors but is essential

Reading Jesus' Parables with Dao De Jing

to the life of all. "Water is the best thing in the world" (shǎng shàn ruò shuǐ). Simply, water serves all; therefore, it is close to the Dao. In Dao De Jing 52, we also see the importance of softness/weakness as in water. Shǒu róu yuē jiàng means "to keep softness is the strength." Water is soft and weak. Because of that, it is strong. The ideal way of life is to be like water, which is soft (chapters 3–4, 10, 36, 43, 52, 55–56, 58, 76, 78) and weak (chapters 29, 36, 55, 76, 78). A virtuous person is like a newborn infant whose bones are soft and muscles are weak, and yet their grip is secure. Those who maintain softness are strong and conquer themselves. This idea is expressed with zì shèng zhě jiàng, which means: "The wise conquer themselves and therefore they are strong" (33). Those who conquer others are forceful, but those who conquer themselves are strong. Also in Dao De Jing 40, there is ruò zhě dào zhī yòng, which means: "To be soft or weak is the function of the Way" (40).

Father and Two Sons (Luke 15:11–32)

11 Then Jesus said, "There was a man who had two sons. 12 The younger of them said to his father, 'Father, give me the share of the property that will belong to me.' So he divided his property between them. 13 A few days later the younger son gathered all he had and traveled to a distant country, and there he squandered his property in dissolute living. 14 When he had spent everything, a severe famine took place throughout that country, and he began to be in need. 15 So he went and hired himself out to one of the citizens of that country, who sent him to his fields to feed the pigs. 16 He would gladly have filled himself with the pods that the pigs were eating; and no one gave him anything. 17 But when he came to himself he said, 'How many of my father's hired hands have bread enough and to spare, but here I am dying of hunger! 18 I will get up and go to my father, and I will say to him, "Father, I have sinned against heaven and before you; 19 I am no longer worthy to be called your son; treat me like one of your hired hands."' 20 So he set off and went to his father. But while he was still far off, his father

Parables from the Perspective of "Softness/Weakness"

saw him and was filled with compassion; he ran and put his arms around him and kissed him. 21 Then the son said to him, 'Father, I have sinned against heaven and before you; I am no longer worthy to be called your son.' 22 But the father said to his slaves, 'Quickly, bring out a robe— the best one— and put it on him; put a ring on his finger and sandals on his feet. 23 And get the fatted calf and kill it, and let us eat and celebrate; 24 for this son of mine was dead and is alive again; he was lost and is found!' And they began to celebrate. 25 "Now his elder son was in the field; and when he came and approached the house, he heard music and dancing. 26 He called one of the slaves and asked what was going on. 27 He replied, 'Your brother has come, and your father has killed the fatted calf, because he has got him back safe and sound.' 28 Then he became angry and refused to go in. His father came out and began to plead with him. 29 But he answered his father, 'Listen! For all these years I have been working like a slave for you, and I have never disobeyed your command; yet you have never given me even a young goat so that I might celebrate with my friends. 30 But when this son of yours came back, who has devoured your property with prostitutes, you killed the fatted calf for him!' 31 Then the father said to him, 'Son, you are always with me, and all that is mine is yours. 32 But we had to celebrate and rejoice, because this brother of yours was dead and has come to life; he was lost and has been found.'"

The story of the Father and Two Son is about a dysfunctional family. The main character is the father whose heart was broken and weak due to his younger son's immature behavior. He appears to be mother-like and has a weak image throughout the story. He waits for his son outside of his house and hugs and kisses upon his return. The father's response to his son is seen very weak and soft. He behaves very unconventionally and risks his honor as a typical father in a village. All he wants is to restore family. Justice can be done after that. The problem of the older brother is that he has a "hard" heart. He does not understand his father's feast for his younger brother. The father responds to his older son: "For this *your brother* was dead, and is alive; he was lost, and is found" (Luke 15:32). Certainly, the older brother's view is not wrong because justice is also important. If someone does wrong, he/she must be punished. He cannot understand his younger brother's immature action that he betrayed his family, wasting the family property. He serves as a prosecutor. But the only thing he lacks is a "soft or weak" heart that is had by his father who knows what is the priority, which is to accept his younger son with mercy. Justice can be done after that. The father welcomes his son not because he repented or did a good thing. Even before his son came back, the father was ready to accept him because he had an unconditional love for him.

Pharisee and Tax-Collector (Luke 18:9–14)

> *9 He also told this parable to some who trusted in themselves that they were righteous and regarded others with contempt:* 10 "Two men went up to the temple to pray, one a Pharisee and the other a tax collector. 11 The Pharisee, standing by himself, was praying thus, 'God, I thank you that I am not like other people: thieves, rogues, adulterers, or even like this tax collector. 12 I fast twice a week; I give a tenth of all my income.' 13 But the tax collector, standing far off, would not even look up to heaven, but was beating his breast and saying, 'God, be merciful to me, a sinner!' 14 I tell you, this man went down to his home justified rather than the other; *for all who exalt themselves will be humbled, but all who humble themselves will be exalted.*" (Italics indicate the Lukan addition to the parable proper).

In the Parable of Pharisee and Tax-collector, the Pharisee utters a very standard prayer, as in the Talmud: "I give thanks to thee, O Lord my God, that thou hast given me my lot with those who sit in the seat of learning, and not with those who sit at the street corners; for I am early to work, and they are early to work; I am early to work on words of the Torah and they are early to

Parables from the Perspective of "Softness/Weakness"

work on things of no moment."[1] He feels great about himself because he does well in keeping the law. On the one hand, he is not a hypocrite. But on the other hand, the problems is that he does not have any pity toward those sinners. He feels superior to others who are unlike him. He lacks a "soft/weak" mind that inquires about their miserable status. Thus he could pray like this: "God, what is wrong with them? What can I do for them? Have mercy on them." In contrast, the tax-collector says a very simple, desperate prayer that reveals his nothingness before God: "God, be merciful to me, a sinner!" (Luke 18:13).[2] His prayer echoes Psalm 51: "Have mercy on me, God, in your goodness; in your abundant compassion blot out my offense." He was evil in society, but now he turns to God with a broken heart. He begins to take the first step toward a good righteous relationship with God. What God wants is not self-righteousness but a humbling spirit that searches for God.

---

1. Talmud, b. Ber 28b. Similarly in Qumran Thanksgiving Hymns, 1QH 7:34; 15:34.

2. In Dao De Jing 81: "True words are not beautiful. Beautiful words are not truthful."

5

Parables from the Perspective of "Gravity"

Dao De Jing 25

There was something of the chaotic whole before heaven and earth were born: the silent, formless, complete, and unchanging. It spreads everywhere, benefiting all. It is the mother of all things. I do not know its name; I just call it the Way. If I have to describe it, the only word I can utter is "great." Great means outgoing and outgoing means reaching far. Reaching far means return. Thus the Way is great. Heaven is great, the earth is great, and the king is also great. Among four things great in the world is humanity. Humanity follows earth. Earth follows heaven. Heaven follows the Way. The Way follows nature.

Dao De Jing 26

Gravity is the root of lightness. Calmness wins over hastiness. Therefore, while traveling all day, the wise do not leave the baggage-wagons. Though seeing gorgeous

Parables from the Perspective of "Gravity"

things, they stay calm and are indifferent to them. How can the lords with ten thousand chariots allow themselves to be lighter than the world? To be light is to lose the root. To be in haste is to lose self-control.

In Dao De Jing 25, the Dao (Way) is the source of all. It is everywhere and complete. It can reach far and ongoing. But reaching far means a return to earth. That is, people need to follow earth (rén fǎ de), which represents "gravity or calm." In Dao De Jing 26, there is "chóng wéi qīng gēn," which means: "Gravity is the root of lightness." In nature, heaviness or gravity supports the light parts, as the root of a tree buttresses the whole tree.

Rich Fool (Luke 12:16–21)

16 The land of a rich man produced abundantly. 17 And he thought to himself, 'What should I do, for I have no place to store my crops?' 18 Then he said, 'I will do this: I will pull down my barns and build larger ones, and there I will store all my grain and my goods. 19 And I will say to my soul, 'Soul, you have ample goods laid up for many years; relax, eat, drink, be merry.' 20 But God said to him, 'You fool! This very night your life is being demanded of you. And the things you have prepared, whose will they be?' 21 So it is with those who store up treasures for themselves but are not rich toward God.

In the Parable of Rich Fool, a rich man does not know how he became rich. The land along with other conditions produced abundantly. Also, there were people who worked for him in his land. Like the root of a tree, there were things and people that supported him. Moreover, from God's perspective, the land is not his but given to all. The rich man does not have a calm mind and focuses on himself: "What should I do, for I have no place to store my crops?" However, the right question must be: How can I distribute them to others because I have too many? If he knew how he became rich, he would thank all those who worked for him. What he has to pull down is not his warehouse but his self-centered heart. Then God said to him, "You fool! This very night your life is being demanded of you. And the things you have prepared, whose will they be?" The rich fool must return to calm.

Unmerciful Servant (Matt 18:23-35)

> 23 For this reason the kingdom of heaven may be compared to a king who wished to settle accounts with his slaves. 24 When he began the reckoning, one who owed him ten thousand talents was brought to him; 25 and, as he could not pay, his lord ordered him to be sold, together with his wife and children and all his possessions, and payment to be made. 26 So the slave fell on his knees before him, saying, 'Have patience with me, and I will pay you everything.' 27 And out of pity for him, the lord of that slave released him and forgave him the debt. 28 But that same slave, as he went out, came upon one of his fellow slaves who owed him a hundred denarii; and seizing him by the throat, he said, 'Pay what you owe.' 29 Then his fellow slave fell down and pleaded with him, 'Have patience with me, and I will pay you.' 30 But he refused; then he went and threw him into prison until he would pay the debt. 31 When his fellow slaves saw what had happened, they were greatly distressed, and they went and reported to their lord all that had taken place. 32 Then his lord summoned him and said to him, 'You wicked slave! I forgave you all that debt because you pleaded with me. 33 Should you not have had mercy on your fellow slave, as I had mercy on you?' 34 And in anger his lord handed him over to be tortured until he would pay his entire debt. 35 So my heavenly Father will also do to every one of you, if you do not forgive your brother or sister from your heart.

In the Parable of the Unmerciful Servant, there is a story about a certain slave whose huge debt (ten thousand talents, which is the incalculable amount of money) was forgiven. But he does not forgive his fellow slave's small debt (only a hundred denarii). He was overjoyed at his huge debt cancelled. He may have thought that he was so lucky. But soon he forgot about the grace he received from his king. Probably, he was forgiven too fast to forgive his friend's small debt. He had to remember his own miserable status when he needed a desperate help from his king and must support his friend by forgiving his small debt. He even does not know that he may fall again into debt. In a scary world, what is needed is mutual care and support. That is a mind of calm, which is the root of a tree that supports the whole tree.

6

Parables from the Perspective of "Lowliness"

Dao De Jing 6

The spirit of the valley does not die. It is called a mystical mother. Her womb is the root of heaven and earth. It looks like a barely continuous valley, but it ever exists. Though used all the time, it is inexhaustible.

Dao De Jing 66

Rivers and seas can be lords of the hundred valleys because they lower themselves to them; therefore, they can be lords of all the valleys. So to be above people, you must speak humbly to them. To lead them, you must place yourself behind them. When the wise are above, people do not feel burdened; when they are ahead, people are not hindered. Therefore, the world is pleased with them and never tires of them. Because they do not compete, the world cannot compete with them.

Parables from the Perspective of "Lowliness"

In Dao De Jing 6, valley as a metaphor signifies "lowliness" in the human attitude and work. Whereas mountain takes pride in its height, valley remains low in shade and calm. Valleys are channels of water, sending it to rivers and seas. Valley is called a mystical mother because it produces and nurtures life. In Dao De Jing 66 as well, there is a similar theme of lowliness. Water flows from the higher to the lower places. Many drops of rain come down the mountains and make streams and valleys. The Way is like rivers; it never claims greatness, and therefore it is great (Dao De Jing 32).

Rich Man and Lazarus (Luke 16:19-31)

19 There was a rich man who was dressed in purple and fine linen and who feasted sumptuously every day. 20 And at his gate lay a poor man named Lazarus, covered with sores, 21 who longed to satisfy his hunger with what fell from the rich man's table; even the dogs would come and lick his sores. 22 The poor man died and was carried away by the angels to be with Abraham. The rich man also died and was buried. 23 In Hades, where he was being tormented, he looked up and saw Abraham far away with Lazarus by his side. 24 He called out, 'Father Abraham, have mercy on me, and send Lazarus to dip the tip of his finger in water and cool my tongue; for I am in agony in these flames.' 25 But Abraham said, 'Child, remember that during your lifetime you received your good things, and Lazarus in like manner evil things; but now he is comforted here, and you are in agony. 26 Besides all this, between you and us a great chasm has been fixed, so that those who might want to pass from here to you cannot do so, and no one can cross from there to us.' 27 He said, 'Then, father, I beg you to send him to my father's house— 28 for I have five brothers— that he may warn them, so that they will not also come into this place of torment.' 29 Abraham replied, 'They have Moses and the prophets; they should listen to them.' 30 He said, 'No, father Abraham; but if someone goes to them from the dead, they will repent.' 31 He said to him, 'If they do

not listen to Moses and the prophets, neither will they be convinced even if someone rises from the dead.'

In the Parable of the Rich Man and Lazarus, we can suppose that a rich man reached mountaintop in terms of his career because he has a sumptuous feast every day with his friends. We do not know how he became rich, but one thing we know for sure is that he did not notice or care for a poor man named Lazarus, lying at his gate, with sores covering his body. His busy, successful life prevented him from seeing a poor person who needed a desperate help. He should have come out of his house and had to meet Lazarus who was struggling to survive in the lowest valley of his life. If he had done so, he could have saved Lazarus. Perhaps we could have known his name. But he thought his success was measured by riches and a number of "good" friends coming to his party. But his real success is measured by his service to the lowly people in the valley.

Good Samaritan (Luke 10:30-37)

30 Jesus replied, "A man was going down from Jerusalem to Jericho, and fell into the hands of robbers, who stripped him, beat him, and went away, leaving him half dead. 31 Now by chance a priest was going down that road; and when he saw him, he passed by on the other side. 32 So likewise a Levite, when he came to the place and saw him, passed by on the other side. 33 But a Samaritan while traveling came near him; and when he saw him, he was moved with pity. 34 He went to him and bandaged his wounds, having poured oil and wine on them. Then he put him on his own animal, brought him to an inn, and took care of him. 35 The next day he took out two denarii, gave them to the innkeeper, and said, 'Take care of him; and when I come back, I will repay you whatever more you spend.' 36 Which of these three, do you think, was a neighbor to the man who fell into the hands of the robbers?" 37 He said, "The one who showed him mercy." Jesus said to him, "Go and do likewise."

Parables from the Perspective of "Lowliness"

In the Parable of the Good Samaritan, a priest and a Levite passed by a victim and did not check what happened to that man. Even if they knew what happened to him, they decided to pass by. Now a Samaritan came to the scene and stopped to check him, half-dead on a dangerous road. But "he was moved with pity." He did all things he could. First of all, he did not avoid him or pass by, but "he went to him." In order to approach him, he got off from his animal. Then he used all he had and served the victim with them. He bandaged his wounds and poured oil and wine on them. Then "he put him on his own animal," which means giving his seat to him. He put the victim on his place on his animal. Then he brought him to an inn and took care of him. He gave full service to him, becoming a valley of the world to the one half-dead in a valley. He crossed the religious and ethnic boundary and helped the victim without discrimination. He was like water, flowing into a lowly place. Nothing could prevent him from stretching his hands out to the needy.

7

Conclusion

Even if we live in a most technological age, the basic human conditions have not changed much from the first century CE. We still ask today: "What is a good life? What is wrong with humanity? What is an alternative wisdom that we can explore? What can we do to make a justice society?" In this concluding chapter, I put a list of ten most important lessons from the parables of Jesus. The corresponding chapters of the Dao De Jing may be read together with the parables. With these lessons, readers will make their own detailed lesson plan. See below the ten lessons of the parables.

1. Sow seeds to the ground as widely as possible without discrimination
Sower
*Dao De Jing 5, 49

2. Know that you cannot do all
Seed Growing Secretly
*Dao De Jing 71

Conclusion

3. Acknowledge the coexistence of good and evil
Wheat and Weed
*Dao De Jing 74

4. See the hidden potential
Leaven
*Dao De Jing 66

5. See the power of small
Mustard Seed
*Dao De Jing 52

6. Think from other person's perspective
Vineyard Workers, Good Samaritan
*Dao De Jing 22, 25, 40, 45, 77

7. Do not compete with others; find a way to live together
Father and Two Sons, Pharisee and Tax Collector
*Dao De Jing 8

8. Find the most valuable and live with it
Pearl
*Dao De Jing 56

9. Do your best without fear
The Parable of Talents
*Dao De Jing 13, 50

10. Do not fill your mind
Rich Fool, Empty Jar (Gospel of Thomas)
*Dao De Jing 3, 9, 15

Appendix

A New Translation of the Dao De Jing

As is the case with classical studies, we do not have the original text of the Dao De Jing. There are multiple versions of the Dao De Jing. However, I decided not to deal with textual matters in my translation. This translation is based on the Wang Bi version, one of the most widely-held authoritative texts. The typical translation of the beginning verse is as follows: "The Dao that can be told is not the permanent truth." However, my translation is different: "The Way is manifested as a way, and it is not fixed." The problem for Laozi is not that there is no permanent truth in this world but that people do not practice the Dao (Way) even if they know.

1
There was no name when heaven and earth started[1]
The Way is manifested as a way, but it is not fixed.
Name is a name, but it is not fixed.
There was no name when heaven and earth started.
Name was given to call things in the world.

---

1. There is no title in the Dao De Jing. I made it for the convenient purpose.

Appendix

Therefore, always without desire, we see a deep mystery of things in the world.
Always with desire, we see their manifestations.
The two are from the same source but have different names.
This sameness is called deep mystery, mystery upon mystery, the gate to all mystery.

2
Teach without words

We see the beautiful as beautiful because we presuppose something not beautiful.
We see the good as good because we presuppose something not good.
Therefore, being and non-being exist by its relation.
Difficult and easy exist by its relative difficulty.
Long and short exist by its comparison.
High and low is decided by its slope.
Instrumental sound and voice are harmonized by its relation.
Front and back depend on its place.
The wise act with non-arbitrary action. Teach without words.
Acknowledge that all things run their course. Produce things, but do not possess them.
You can accomplish things, but do not depend on them. Because of this, your works will last long.

3
Do not praise those who are smart

Do not praise those who are smart. Then people will not rival with each other.
Do not value treasures that are difficult to obtain. Then people will not become robbers.
Do not show things that stimulate people to want. Then people will not be disturbed by them.
Therefore, the wise live by controlling their minds.
Let people empty their hearts and fill their bellies.
Let them soften their will and strengthen their bones of action.

Let them have no selfish knowledge and self-centered desire.
Help them do things by the course of nature.
If things are done naturally, nothing would be impossible to govern.

4
Become one with the dust
The Way is like an empty bowl; it is used up but inexhaustible.
It is like a deep pond, the source of all things.
It blunts the sharp. It unties the entangled.
It softens the splendid. Become one with the dust.
The Way is seen in depth and calm.
I do not understand how the Way (Dao) began.
It must have been before the heaven and earth.

5
Heaven and earth are impartial
Heaven and earth are impartial.
They treat all things as straw dogs.
The wise are also impartial.
They treat people as straw dogs.
Heaven and earth are like a bellows.
While empty, it is never exhausted.
The more it is worked, the more it produces.
Much talk counts little.
Keep focused on the inside of you.

6
The spirit of the valley does not die
The spirit of the valley does not die. It is called a mystical mother.
Her womb is the root of heaven and earth.
It looks like a barely continuous valley, but it ever exists.
Though used all the time, it is inexhaustible.

Appendix

7
Heaven and earth are big, lasting long
Heaven and earth are big, lasting long because they do not live for themselves.
The wise put themselves behind; therefore, they advance.
Giving up themselves, they find themselves.
Giving up selfish desire, they fulfill themselves.

8
Water is the best thing in the world
Water is the best thing in the world.
It benefits all things without competing with them.
It flows to lower places that people do not want to go.
Therefore, it is closest to the Way.
Look for lowly places. Look into the depth of all things.
Treat others with mercy. Speak trusting words.
Do right things when governing. Act mercifully and timely.
Do not compete with others and there will be no fault with you.

9
Leaving a vessel unfilled is better than filling it
Leaving a vessel unfilled is better than filling it.
Things too sharp do not last long.
A full load of gold and jade in a house will not be kept safe.
Wealth and fame bring arrogance and calamity to people.
When good work is accomplished, leave it. That is the Way of heaven.

10
Give birth to and nourish all things in the world
Can you hold soul and body together so that they won't be separated?
Can you become an infant if you have the softness of breath?
Can you cleanse your heart and make it flawless?
Can you love people and govern the nation without arbitrary knowledge?

Can you become a mystic woman who opens the gate of heaven?
Can you lighten the neighborhood without arbitrary action?
Give birth to and nourish all things in the world.
Produce them without possessing. Complete them, but do not rely on them.
Take care, but do not dominate them. This is called deep virtue.

11
The usefulness of the room depends on its empty space
Thirty spokes are joined to the hub of a wheel; but the usefulness of the wheel depends on the empty space between the hub and the rim.
Clay is used to making a vessel, but the usefulness of the vessel depends on its empty space.
Doors and windows are cut out to make a room; but the usefulness of the room depends on its empty space. Therefore, the tangible has benefits, but the intangible makes it useful.

12
The five colors blind your eyes
The five colors blind your eyes.
The five tones deafen your ears.
The five flavors dull your taste.
Horse-racing and hunting drive you crazy.
The rare and precious goods-to-obtain make you astray.
Therefore, the wise take care of the belly, but not the eyes.
They accept the one and reject the other.

13
Regard the world as precious as your body
Take both disgrace and honor as a pleasant surprise.
Regard trouble and suffering as precious as your body.
What does "taking disgrace and honor as a pleasant surprise" mean?
It means you have to be humble.
If things are going well, you are surprised with thanks.

Appendix

Even if things are not going well, you are surprised because you can learn from failure.
What does "regarding trouble and suffering as precious as your body" mean? It means we suffer because we are a body.
How can I suffer if I have no body?
If you regard the world as precious as your body, you are entrusted to work for the world.
If you love the world as your body, you can take care of the world.

14
Realities in the world are infinite and unnamable
We look at it and do not see it. We call it invisible.
We listen to it and do not hear it. We call it inaudible.
We touch it and do not hold it. We call it intangible.
These three cannot be fully comprehended; Therefore, they merge into one.
Things on the higher place are not brighter than on other places.
Things on the lower place are not darker than on other places.
Realities in the world are infinite and unnamable.
They return to the status of nothingness when there was no name.
It is the formless form and the imageless image.
This is called a mysterious enlightenment.
You greet and face a person, and do not see his or her head.
You follow after a person and do not see his or her back.
If you live today by following the Way of old wisdom,
there will be a new life. You will understand the Way.

15
The profound wisdom of the wise is too deep or subtle to comprehend
The profound wisdom of the wise is too deep or subtle to comprehend.
Because it is beyond our comprehension, it can be only described by its appearance.
It is like a hesitating person in crossing a thinly frozen stream in the winter.

Like a person at a loss when surrounded by people.
Like a guest who is cautious.
Like effacing ice in the thaw.
Like uncarved wood.
Like an open valley.
Like the mixed muddy water.
Who can gradually clear the muddy water?
Who can stay calm and help others to get back to dynamic life?
Those who abide by the Way do not fill their desires.
Because they do not seek their desires, they complete works.

16
Empty your mind thoroughly and keep yourself calm
Empty your mind thoroughly and keep yourself calm.
Then you will see all things arising and returning.
Though all are flourishing, they return to the root.
To return to the root is called tranquility.
It means returning to destiny.
Returning to destiny is the constant law.
To know this constant is enlightenment.
If you do not know this, your life will be miserable or delusive.
If you know this constant, you are open-minded and embrace all.
If you embrace all, you are impartial.
To be impartial means to be justice-minded.
To be justice-minded is to be under heaven.
To be under heaven is to be one with the Way.
To be one with the Way is to last forever.
There is no fear of death.

17
The best leader is the one who people barely know exists
The best leader is the one who people barely know exists.
The next best is loved and praised. Next comes the one feared.
The worst leader is despised.
If the leader does not trust people, they will not put faith in the leader.

The wise utter a few precious and cautious words.
When things go well and bear fruit, people will say, "We have done it ourselves, as we do in nature."

18
When the great way is forsaken, codes of morality and justice arise

When the great way is forsaken, codes of morality and justice arise.
If knowledge and intelligence are rampant, the great hypocrisy emerges.
When family relationships are not in harmony, filial piety and parental kindness are emphasized.
When a country falls into chaos, loyal patriots appear.

19
Forget holiness and abandon intelligence

Forget holiness and abandon intelligence.
People will benefit a hundredfold.
Abandon morality and discard codes of justice.
People will return to natural love.
Abandon sly skills and do not seek profit.
There will be no thieves or robbers.
These three things are needed, but not sufficient.
The following are essential:
Be simple or authentic like uncarved wood.
See you are small and temper your desires.

20
Do not pursue ambitious knowledge

Do not pursue ambitious knowledge. Your sorrows will end.
How much difference is there between "yes" and "no"?
How much difference is there between good and evil?
Should I fear what others fear?
That is a barren, pointless thought.

People are merry, ascending a tower in the spring time as though at a holiday feast.
I alone am inactive with no desires like an infant who has not smiled yet.
I appear weary and feel no home to which to return.
People possess more than they need; I alone have nothing.
I must be a fool, and am confused. Other people are bright;
I alone am dark. People are clever; I alone am dull.
I drift as the sea, like the wind without a destination.
People have a purpose; I alone am stubborn and uncouth.
Though I am different from others,
I value drawing sustenance from the Way of the mother.

21
The great way seems elusive and evasive
The power of great virtue comes from following a great way.
The great way seems elusive and evasive.
Evasive and elusive!
Yet an image is within itself.
Elusive and evasive!
Yet a substance is within itself.
Subtle and obscure!
Yet there is a core of life within itself.
Its core is real and reliable.
From ancient times until now, its name stayed the same, and all beings have come from it.
How do I know the beginning of all? By these!

22
To yield means to be whole
To yield means to be whole.
To be bent means to be straight.
To be empty means to be full.
To be worn out means to be renewed.
To have little means to gain.
To have plenty means to be perplexed.

Therefore, the wise embrace the whole and become a beacon of the world.
They do not display themselves and therefore they are illumined.
They do not claim themselves and therefore they are distinguished.
They do not boast of themselves and therefore they endure long.
They do not compete, and therefore the world does not compete with them.
Therefore, the old saying of "to yield means to be whole" is not hollow words.
Strive to be whole and all things will flow naturally.

23
Nature says few words
Nature says few words.
A whirlwind does not last all morning.
A downpour of rain endures no whole day.
This is the work of heaven.
How much more unpredictable are humans than heaven!
Therefore, the one who follows the Way is one with the Way.
The one who follows virtue is one with virtue.
The one who follows loss is one with the loss.
Therefore, the one who is one with the Way is happy because of the Way.
The one who is one with virtue is happy because of virtue.
The one who is one with loss is happy because of loss.
If you lack trust, you will not be trusted.

24
Those who stand on tiptoes cannot stand firm
Those who stand on tiptoes cannot stand firm.
Those who take too great a stride cannot go forward.
Those who show off cannot shine forth.
Those who assert their views are not distinguished.
Those who boast of their accomplishments are not given credit.
Those who assert their greatness cannot endure for long.

From the perspective of the Way, all these things are useless like extra food or waste.
No one likes them; therefore, do not adhere to them.

25
The Way follows nature
There was something of the chaotic whole before heaven and earth were born: the silent, formless, complete, and unchanging.
It spreads everywhere, benefiting all. It is the mother of all things.
I do not know its name; I just call it the Way.
If I have to describe it, the only word I can utter is "great."
Great means outgoing and outgoing means reaching far.
Reaching far means return. Thus the Way is great.
Heaven is great, the earth is great, and the king is also great.
Among four things great in the world is humanity.
Humanity follows earth.
Earth follows heaven.
Heaven follows the Way.
The Way follows nature.

26
Gravity is the root of lightness
Gravity is the root of lightness.
Calmness wins over hastiness.
Therefore, while traveling all day, the wise do not leave the baggage-wagons.
Though seeing gorgeous things, they stay calm and are indifferent to them.
How can the lords with ten thousand chariots allow themselves to be lighter than the world?
To be light is to lose the root.
To be in haste is to lose self-control.

27
A good traveler leaves no tracks
A good traveler leaves no tracks.

Appendix

A good speaker has no flaws to censure.
A good accountant needs no counters.
A well-shut door needs no bars or bolts.
A well-tied knot needs no rope, and yet it cannot be untied.
Therefore, those who live according to the Way are good at saving people;
nobody is abandoned.
They are also good at saving things;
nothing is wasted.
This is called awakening wisdom.
Therefore, the good teach the bad,
and the bad is the material from which the good may learn.
If people do not respect the teacher or do not find lessons to learn,
They are greatly deluded no matter how learned they are.
This is the essence of enlightenment.

28
Know the masculine and keep to the feminine

Know the masculine and keep to the feminine.
Become the valley of the world.
If you become the valley of the world,
you will abide in eternal virtue and return to infancy.
Know the white and keep to the black.
Become a model for the world.
If you become a model for the world,
You will abide in eternal virtue and return to primordial nothingness.
Know the glorious and keep the lowly.
Become the valley of the world.
Then you will abide in virtue and return to the state of the uncarved wood.
The uncarved wood is carved to be instrumented.
The wise carve and transform it into leaders.
The great ruler does not break or divide it up.

29
The wise avoid extremes, excesses, and extravagances
If you try to take over and manipulate the world, you won't succeed.
The world is a sacred vessel, and you cannot control it.
If you try to do so, you would destroy it.
If you try to hold it, you will lose it.
For all things in the world, some may go ahead, and others follow behind.
There are times for breathing slowly and for breathing fast.
There are times to grow in strength and to be in weakness.
There are times to ascend and to descend.
Therefore, the wise avoid extremes, excesses, and extravagances.

30
What is against the Way will soon come to an end
Those who assist the ruler according to the Way should not try to rule the world by force of arms.
Such action rebounds.
Wherever armies are stationed, thorns and brambles grow.
After a great war, there will be years of famine.
The wise do what has to be done, and know when to stop.
They do not press upon victory.
They achieve the purpose, but they do not brag about it.
In completing their work, they are not haughty.
Accomplishing their work, they do not dominate others.
If things in the world overdevelop, they will decay fast because it is not the Way.
What is against the Way will soon come to an end.

31
Those who follow the Way do not set their mind on them
Fine weapons are not favorable instruments and detested by people.
Those who follow the Way do not set their mind on them.
Therefore, in domestic affairs, the rulers honor the left side that represents peace.

Appendix

But at times of war, they honor the right side that represents emergency management.
Weapons are not good instruments, and the rulers should not strive for them.
If it is unavoidable to use them, they must be used with utmost restraint.
Even if they are victorious, they do not praise their victory.
To praise victory is to delight in killing people.
Those who delight in killing humanity will fail in the country.
In good times, the left side is honored.
In bad times, the right side is honored.
The lieutenant general stands on the left.
The senior general stands on the right.
This arrangement is due to funeral ceremonies.
If many people are killed at war, there must be sorrow and grief.
Even victory at war must be treated as a funeral ceremony.

32
The Way is nameless like the small uncarved wood
The Way is nameless like the small uncarved wood.
Yet no one in the world can control or master it.
If the rulers stick to the way of life, the world will serve them spontaneously.
Heaven and earth will act in harmony and sprinkle sweet dew.
People will be at peace with no one giving orders.
Once the uncarved block is carved, names will appear.
As soon as there are names, know that it is time to stop.
If you know when it is time to stop, you would not be endangered.
The Way in the world is like rivers and streams flowing into the sea.

33
Those who know themselves are enlightened
Those who know others are clever.
Those who know themselves are enlightened.
Those who conquer others are forceful.
Those who conquer themselves are strong.

Those who are content are rich.
Those who act with vigor are willful.
Those who do not lose their place will endure.
Those who die without perishing will last long.

34
The great way of life is like a river
The great way of life is like a river of which its overflowing water
    goes to the left and right.
All things depend on it for life, and it does not turn away from them.
The Way accomplishes its work but does not claim credit for it.
It provides for and nourishes all things, but is not master over them.
It does not seek its own will and is small.
All things come to it, but it does not control them.
It never claims greatness, and therefore it is great.

35
The words of the Way are insipid and tasteless
Hold fast to the great form of the Way, and the world will run with
    no harm.
It will come in peace, comfort, and security.
Music and food can make passing travelers stop.
But the words of the Way are insipid and tasteless.
It is invisible to eyes. It is inaudible to ears.
It is inexhaustible to practice.

36
What is soft and weak can overcome what is hard and strong
To contract something, you must first stretch it.
To weaken something, you must first make it strong.
If you want to tear down something, you must first raise it up.
To take something, you must first give it. This is called subtle
    illumination.
What is soft and weak can overcome what is hard and strong.
As fish should not leave the water, sharp weapons of the state should
    not be shown to the people.

Appendix

37
The way of simple diversity like the nameless uncarved wood

The Way of life is not to seek one's own will.
But nothing cannot be accomplished.
If leaders of the state live according to the Way, the world will be reformed spontaneously.
Against the desire of seeking my will, I will follow the potential of the nameless uncarved wood.
Because it does not seek its own will, there is tranquility.
The world will find peace of its own accord.

38
When the Way is lost, virtue arises

Those who are virtuous do not care about virtue.
Therefore, they have virtue.
Those who are not virtuous care about virtue.
Therefore, they have no virtue.
Those who are virtuous do not do things by their arbitrary will.
They do not find reasons to do so.
Those who are not virtuous do things by their arbitrary will.
They find reasons to do so.
Humanitarian people do things by their arbitrary will.
They find no reasons to do so.
Moral people do things by their arbitrary will.
They find reasons to do so.
Courteous people do things by their arbitrary will.
If their will is not heard, they roll up their sleeves and force others to follow their custom.
Therefore, when the Way is lost, virtue arises.
When virtue is lost, humanity arises.
When humanity is lost, custom arises.
Custom is the husk of loyalty and faithfulness; it is the beginning of disorder.

Foreknowledge is the flower of the Way and the beginning of foolishness.
Therefore. mature people dwell in the thick of the Way and do not rest with the thin.
They dwell in the fruit and do not rest with the flower. What matters is fruit.

39
Great leaders will fail without proper character and action
From ancient times there is oneness in the world.
Heaven is clear according to this principle of oneness.
Earth is stable according to this principle of oneness.
Spirits are divine according to this principle of oneness.
Valleys are full according to this principle of oneness.
All things in the world exist and grow according to this principle of oneness.
People become great leaders of the world according to this principle of oneness.
All these are possible because there is a principle of oneness.
Heaven would be split without that which clarifies it.
Earth would be unstable without that which makes it stable.
Spirits would be inanimate without that which makes it divine.
Valleys would be exhausted without that which makes it full.
All things would not exist without that which makes them exist.
Great leaders will fail without proper character and action.
Therefore, lowliness is the basis for nobility.
The low is the basis for the high.
Great leaders will consider themselves orphans, widows, and the poor.
I mean this that lowliness is the basis for nobility.
Therefore, too much glory means no glory.
Do not be like the glittering jade, but be like a common stone.

40
Reversion is the movement of the Way
Reversion is the movement of the Way.

Appendix

Weakness is the function of the Way.
All things in the world come from being.
Being comes from non-being.

41
A great vessel takes time to be filled
When the wise person hears of the Way, they act it out diligently.
When the mediocre hear of the Way,
they are uncertain and do not practice it.
When the foolish hear of the Way, they laugh out loud.
If it were not laughed at, it would not be the Way.
Therefore, there is an old saying:
"The enlightenment of the Way seems obscure.
Progression in the Way seems like regression.
The even path of the Way seems uneven.
The higher virtue seems like valleys.
Great purity seems tarnished.
Great character seems weak.
Solid virtue seems lacking.
A great space has no corners.
A great vessel takes time to be filled.
A great sound is inaudible.
A great form is shapeless."
The Way is hidden and indescribable.
Yet it alone nourishes and completes all things.

42
Loss is gain
The Way produces one.
One produces two.
Two produces three.
Three produces all things.
All things bear Yin and embrace Yang.
Yin and Yang together produce harmony.
People hate being orphaned, lonely, and poor.
But great leaders call themselves.

Loss is gain. Gain is loss.
What others teach, I also teach:
"Strong and violent people do not die a natural death."
This is the essence of my teaching.

43
The softest things in the world overcome the hardest things
The softest things in the world overcome the hardest things.
Non-being can penetrate even where there is no opening.
By this, I know the benefit of non-forceful action.
Few in the world understand the benefit of wordless teaching and non-forceful action.

44
Those who know when to stop will not fall into danger
Which is dearer, your name or your body?
Which is more important, your body or your wealth?
Which brings more pain, gain or loss?
Therefore, an excessive love for anything will lead to wasteful spending.
Those who hoard most lose most.
Those who are content will not be disgraced.
Those who know when to stop will not fall into danger.
That is the way people can endure and live long.

45
What is most straight seems devious
What is most perfect seems incomplete, but its usefulness is endless.
What is most full seems empty, but its usefulness is endless.
What is most straight seems devious.
Great skill seems clumsy.
Great eloquence seems awkward.
Restlessness overcomes cold, but calm overcomes the heat.
Clarity and stillness are the foundations of the world.

Appendix

46
No fault is greater than the desire to possess
When the world follows the Way, galloping horses are used for tilling the fields.
When the world does not follow the Way, war-horses are bred in the countryside.
No calamity is greater than discontentment.
No fault is greater than the desire to possess.
Know what is enough, and you will be content.

47
The further one goes, the less one knows
One can know the world without going outside.
One can see the Way of heaven without looking out the window.
The further one goes, the less one knows.
Therefore, the wise know without traveling, see without looking and achieve without arbitrary doing.

48
The pursuit of the Way is to unlearn every day
The pursuit of knowledge is to learn or increase something new every day.
The pursuit of the Way is to unlearn every day.
If unlearning takes place, you will act according to the Way, not according to your arbitrary action.
In such a state, nothing will be left undone.
The world is led by non-arbitrary action.
You cannot rule the world according to the unnatural way.

49
The wise have no fixed mind
The wise have no fixed mind; they make the minds of people their mind.
They are good to those who are good.
They are also good to those who are not good.
Goodness is attained.

They act with faith to those who are faithful.
They also act with faith to those who are faithless.
Faithfulness is attained. The wise embrace all.
Therefore, the world will listen to them.
They treat people as their own children.

50
Life is to come out, and death is to enter
Life is to come out; death is to enter.
Three out of ten celebrate life; three out of ten celebrate death; three out of ten simply go from life to death.
What is the reason for this?
It is because of their striving after life.
Some say that those who preserve life well will meet no tigers or wild buffaloes on their road.
They are not harmed by weapons of war.
No buffalo can gore them.
No tiger can claw them.
No weapon can pierce them.
Why is this so? Because they have died, there is no room for death in them.

51
The Way produces them but does not possess them
The Way gives birth to all things, and virtue nurtures them.
Matter forms them, and the environment perfects them.
Therefore, all things respect the Way and value its virtue.
The Way is respected, and virtue is honored.
Not by anyone's order but by the order of nature.
Therefore, the Way produces all things, and virtue nurtures them, caring for them and developing them, sheltering and comforting them, nourishing and protecting them.
The Way produces them but does not possess them.
It helps them but does not rely on them.
It guides them but does not control them.
It is called profound virtue.

Appendix

52
To see small is enlightenment
All things in the world have a beginning, which is called the great mother.
Once we have found the mother, we understand the child.
Once we know the child, we return to keep the mother.
Abiding by the mother, we are free from danger even when the body may die.
Curve your tongue and senses.
You will not be worn out until you die.
If you open your senses with a busier mind and busier activities, you will remain helpless in your life.
To see small is enlightenment.
To keep softness is the strength.
Use the light and return to enlightenment without harming others.
This is the way of practicing the eternal.

53
The great way is smooth and straight
If I have little wisdom, I would walk in a great way.
My only fear would deviate from it.
The great way is smooth and straight; but people prefer devious paths.
The courts are clean and splendid, but the fields are full of weeds.
The storehouses are empty.
Court people wear gorgeous clothes.
They carry fine swords.
They are bored of plenteous food and drink.
They have more possessions than they can use.
This is robbery and extravagance.
It is not from the Way.

54
What is well planted cannot be rooted out
What is well planted cannot be rooted out.

What is firmly held cannot slip away.
Descendants will continue to live honoring the ancestors.
If cultivated in the individual, virtue will become genuine;
If cultivated in the family, virtue will become abundant;
If cultivated in the village, virtue will multiply;
If cultivated in the state, virtue will prosper;
If cultivated in the world, virtue will become universal.
Therefore, observe the individual according to the virtue of the individual.
Observe the family by the family.
Observe the village by the village.
Observe the state by the state.
Observe the world by the world.
How do I know that the world may be so?
By this observation!

55
To extend life unnaturally is ominous
Those who possess virtue in abundance may be compared to newborn infants.
Poisonous creatures will not sting them.
Wild beasts will not seize them.
Predatory birds will not strike them.
Their bones are soft and their muscles are weak.
Yet their grip is secure.
They have never known the union of man and woman, but the organ is fully formed.
They are full of vital energy.
They may cry all day long without getting hoarse.
It is because they are in the perfect harmony.
To know this harmony is the principle of steady life.
To know the principle of steady life means to attain enlightenment.
To extend life unnaturally is ominous.
To manipulate the energy of life is unnatural.
If things are overgrown, they decay because it is not the Way.
Whatever is against the Way soon ceases to be.

Appendix

56
Become one with the dust
Those who know don't talk; those who talk don't know.
Close your mouth and do not rely on your physical senses.
Blunt the sharpness. Untie the tangled.
Soften the brightness. Become one with the dust.
This is a deep awakening of oneness.
Those who live this way are not swayed by friends and enemies,
by benefit and harm, or by honor and disgrace.
Therefore, they are valuable people in the world.

57
I do not force my way
The state can be governed by justice.
Wars can be conducted by surprise tactics.
But the world can be ruled by non-arbitrary action.
How do I know this?
The more prohibitions and taboos in the world, the poorer people will become.
The sharper weapons they have, the more trouble there will be.
The more cunning skills they have, the more extraordinary unnecessary things will be made.
The more rules and regulations, the more thieves and robbers there will be.
Therefore, the wise say:
"I do not force my way, and people will transform themselves.
I maintain serenity, and people will correct themselves.
Because I do not plan things by my way, people will prosper of themselves.
If I do not desire by my way, people will return to the state of the uncarved wood—a mind of simplicity, authenticity, and diversity."

58
When the state is soft and dull, people feel comfortable
When the state is soft and dull, people feel comfortable.

When the state is clever and invasive, people are disappointed and
    treacherous.
Good fortune changes to bad fortune and bad fortune changes to
    good fortune.
Who knows the ultimate end of this process?
Is there no right and wrong?
When justice becomes injustice and goodness become evil, people
    would be confused for a long time.
Therefore, the wise are square but not cornered; they are as sharp as
    a knife but do not cut.
They straighten without straining.
They enlighten without dazzling.

59
To lead people and to serve heaven, you must begin with saving frugality

To lead people and to serve heaven, you must begin with saving
    frugality.
Then you can walk closely in the Way.
If you live with the Way, virtue will be abundant.
With abundant virtue, nothing would be impossible.
There is nothing you cannot overcome, and you can rule the state.
If the state has the mother of the Way, it lives long and strong.
Therefore, roots are to be deep and foundations are to be firm.
That is the way of long enduring life with constant vision.

60
Leading a large country is like cooking a small fish

Leading a large country is like cooking a small fish.
When the world is ruled according to the Way, demons will be
    powerless.
Not that they lose their power but that their power will no longer
    harm people.
As demons do not harm people, the wise do not harm people.
When both do not harm each other, all benefits will spread evenly to
    all people.

Appendix

61
A large state wins over small states by taking the lower position

A large state may be compared to the lower part of a river toward which all streams flow.
It is the converging point of the world; it is the feminine of the world.
The feminine always overcomes the masculine by her quietness.
By stillness, she stays in the low. A large state wins over small states by taking the lower position.
And a small state wins over the large state by acknowledging its lower position.
Some win by placing themselves below, and others win by being below.
While a large state must focus on growing, nurturing, and protecting people,
a small state must admit its lower position and focus on serving people.
Both get what they want. It is best for the large country to place itself below.

62
The Way is treasured by the world

The Way is a sanctuary for creation.
It is a treasure for those who are good; it is a refuge for those who are not good.
Beautiful words can gain honor, but good deeds gain respect from others.
How can we reject others because they are not good?
On crowning an emperor, presenting the Way is better than gifts of rare values.
Why did the ancients value this Way?
Did they not say, "Seek, and you will find?
Though you have sins, you will be forgiven."
Therefore, the Way is treasured by the world.

63
Taste without tasting
Act without interfering.
Do without arbitrary doing.
Taste without tasting.
Regard the small as great.
Regard the few as many.
Repay enmity with virtue.
Deal with the difficult while it is still easy.
Begin great works while they are still small.
Difficult tasks begin with what seems easy, and great accomplishments begin with what is small.
Because the wise try nothing too big, they can accomplish big things.
Those who make easy promises lack faithfulness.
Those who think everything is easy will encounter many difficulties.
The wise always confront difficulties and therefore have no difficulty.

64
A journey of a thousand miles starts with a single step
Things are easier to control while they are quiet.
Things are easier to plan before they manifest omens.
Things break easier while they are still frail.
Things are easier to scatter while they are still small.
Prevent problems before they arise.
Take action before things get too difficult.
The tallest tree begins as a tiny sprout.
A nine-story tower begins with one shovel of dirt.
A journey of a thousand miles starts with a single step.
If you interfere with things and rush into them, you will fail.
If you hold on to things, you will lose them.
The wise do not fail because they do not interfere, leaving things to take their course.
The wise do not lose things because they do not hold on to them.
People usually fail when they are about to succeed.

Appendix

Be as careful of the end by the beginning, and there will be no failure.
Therefore, the wise desire no desire.
They do not value rare treasures.
They learn to unlearn and return to what many have missed so all things may be natural without interference.

65
To rule the country through knowledge harms people
In the old days, those who practiced the Way did not seek to make people clever but aimed at keeping them natural and simple.
People are difficult to govern because they know too much.
To rule the country through knowledge harms people.
To rule the country not through knowledge is a blessing to all.
To understand these two is to understand the ancient standard, which is called deep virtue.
Then virtue becomes deep and far-reaching, and it leads all things back to their original state of great harmony.

66
Rivers and seas can be lords of the hundred valleys because they lower themselves to them
Rivers and seas can be lords of the hundred valleys because they lower themselves to them;
therefore, they can be lords of all the valleys.
So to be above people, you must speak humbly to them.
To lead them, you must place yourself behind them.
When the wise are above, people do not feel burdened;
when they are ahead, people are not hindered.
Therefore, the world is pleased with them and never tires of them.
Because they do not compete, the world cannot compete with them.

67
Love wins all battles
People say my way is great but abnormal.
They say just because it is great, it does not look like the ordinary.

If it were normal, it could have turned small long ago.
I have three treasures to cherish: loving kindness, saving frugality, and a humble mind.
From loving kindness comes courage; from saving frugality comes generosity; from humble mind comes leadership.
Courage without loving kindness, generosity without saving frugality, and leadership without humble mind are fatal.
For love wins all battles and is the strongest defense of all.
Heaven will save and protect those who live with this.

68

Good users of people place themselves below others

Good warriors do not show off their military strength.
Skillful fighters do not become angry.
Skillful conquerors do not compete with people.
Good users of people place themselves below others.
This is called the virtue of not contending.
This is called the power to use people.
This is called attaining harmony with heaven, the highest principle of old.

69

No disaster is greater than underestimating the enemy

There is a saying about war: "I dare not take the offensive but take the defensive.
Rather than advancing an inch, I will retreat a foot."
This means marching without moving, stretching one's arm without showing it, confronting the enemy without meeting, and holding weapons without having them.
No disaster is greater than underestimating the enemy.
Underestimating the enemy means losing all of my greatest assets.
Therefore, when two opposing troops meet in battle, victory belongs to the grieving side.

Appendix

70
The wise wear coarse clothes and keep the jewel inside
My words are easy to understand and put into practice.
Yet no one in the world seems to understand and practice them.
In my words, there is a principle of nature, as there is a center in all things.
Because they do not know this, they do not know me.
Since so few people know me, such understanding is valuable.
Therefore, the wise wear coarse clothes and keep the jewel inside.

71
Knowing not to know is the best
Knowing not to know is the best.
While not knowing, your knowing is a disease.
Only when you recognize the disease as a disease, it is not a disease.
The wise are free from the disease.
Because they recognize the disease as a disease, it is not a disease.

72
Do not restrict their living space
When people do not fear what is dreadful, something dreadful will happen.
Do not restrict their living space.
Do not destroy their livelihoods.
If not burdened by you, they will not bother the leader.
Therefore, the wise persons know themselves, but do not show themselves.
They love themselves, but do not exalt themselves.
So they take one and leave the other.

73
The net of heaven is vast
Those who are brave in daring will perish; those who are brave in not daring will live.
Of these two, one is good, and one is harmful.
Some are not favored by heaven.

Who knows the reason?
Even the wise consider it a difficult question.
The Way of heaven wins without striving.
It gets a good response without speaking.
All needs are met without invoking.
The Way of heaven plans well without haste.
The net of heaven is vast.
Though its meshes are wide, nothing slips through.

74
If people do not fear death
If people do not fear death, how can anybody control them by the threat of death?
Suppose they fear death and we capture and kill those who are law-breakers, who would dare to do so?
There is always an official executioner to deal with this.
If you play the role of the official executioner, it is like cutting wood instead of the master carpenter, and nobody can save their hands from being wounded.

75
Why do people take death lightly?
Why do people get hungry?
They are starving because those above them are taxing too much.
People are difficult to govern because rulers have their own ends in mind.
Why do people take death lightly?
They see death lightly because those above them make too much of life.
People have nothing to live on and find no reason to value such a life.
Those who live by the principle of nature are wiser than those who seek after life.

Appendix

76
The big and strong are laid low; The soft and weak are laid above
When born, people are tender and supple.
At death, they are stiff and hard.
All things are tender and supple while alive.
At death, they wither and dry up.
Therefore, the stiff and hard are companions of death.
The tender and supple are companions of life.
If the army is hard and strong, it will not win.
If a tree is stiff, it will break.
The big and strong are laid low.
The soft and weak are laid above.

77
The Way of heaven reduces what is excessive and supplements what is insufficient
The Way of heaven is like bending a bow.
The upper part is lowered while the lower part is raised.
The excess is reduced and the deficit is increased.
The Way of heaven reduces what is excessive and supplements what is insufficient.
The humanistic way is different. It reduces the insufficient and increases the excessive.
Who can take his or her surplus and give it to the world?
The wise live by the Way.
Therefore, the wise act without expectation.
They do not abide in their accomplishments.
They do not boast of themselves.

78
Nothing in the world is softer and weaker than water
Nothing in the world is softer and weaker than water.
Yet nothing is better for hitting hard and strong things.
There is no substitute for it.
The weak overcomes the strong; the soft overcomes the hard.

All in the world know this, but no one puts it into practice.
Therefore, the wise say whoever suffers disgrace for the country is the owner of the country;
whoever bears the misfortunes of the country is the lord of the world.
True words seem paradoxical.

79
Virtuous people stand in the place of debtors
After settling a massive resentment, there is always an aftermath of resentment.
How can this be deemed as worth?
Therefore, the wise think of the place of a debtor in a business contract and do not blame the other party.
Virtuous people stand in the place of debtors.
Those without virtue exact obligations from others.
The Way of heaven is impartial.
It always stays with the good.

80
A small country with few people is best
A small country with few people is best.
Let people use no complicated machinery.
Let them be mindful of death and not move to distant places.
Although they have boats and chariots, let them have no chance to use them.
Although they have armor and weapons, let them have no chance to use them.
Let people revert to communication by knotting cords.
Help them enjoy food, clothing, and house so they may maintain the simple way of life.
Although people may live so close to the neighboring countries within sight of each other,
hearing the crowing cocks and barking dogs, let them have no travels between them until they die.

Appendix

81
True words are not beautiful

True words are not beautiful.
Beautiful words are not truthful.
The good do not argue for their interest.
Those who argue are not good.
The wise are not erudite.
The erudite are not wise.
The wise do not hoard things.
The more they give to others, the more they have.
The Way of heaven benefits, but does not harm others.
The way of the wise accomplishes without striving.

Resources for Further Study

Borg, Marcus. *Jesus: The Life, Teaching, and Relevance of a Religious Revolutionary*. New York: HaperCollins, 2008.

Buttrick, David. *Speaking Parables: A Homiletic Guide*. Louisville, KY: WJKP, 2000.

Calvin, John. *Commentary on a Harmony of the Evangelists: Matthew, Mark, and Luke* Vol. 3. Edinburgh: Calvin Translation Society, 1846.

Crossan, John Dominic. *In Parables: The Challenge of the Historical Jesus*. New York: Harper & Row, 1973.

De Boer, Martinus. "Ten thousand talents: Matthew's interpretation and redaction of the parable of the Unforgiving Servant(Matt 18:23–35)." *CBQ* 50.2 (1988) 214–232.

Dodd, C.H. (Charles Harold). *The Parables of the Kingdom*. Rev. ed. 1936. London;: James Nisbet & Co.; Fontana, 1961.

Doty, William. "An Interpretation: Parable of the Weeds and Wheat." *Interpretation* 25.2 (1971) 185–193.

Duff, Nancy. "Luke 15:11–32," *Interpretation* 49.1 (1995) 66–69.

Findlay, Alexander. *Jesus and His Parables*. London: Epworth Press, 1950.

Fox, Eric. "The Parable of the Lost or Wandering Sheep: Matthew 18:10–14; Luke 15:3–7." *Anglican Theological Review* 44.1 (1962) 44–57.

Funk, Robert W. *The Parables of Jesus*. Polebridge Press, 1988.

———. "Beyond Criticism in Quest of Literacy: the Parable of the Leaven," *Interpretation* 25.2 (1971) 149–170.

———. "The Good Samaritan as Metaphor." *Semeia* 2 (1974): 74–81.

Funk, Robert W., Bernard Brandon Scott, and James R. Butts, eds. *The Parables of Jesus: Red Letter Edition: A Report of the Jesus Seminar*. Sonoma, Calif.: Polebridge Press, 198

Gowler, David B. *What Are They Saying About the Parables?* New York; Mahwah: Paulist Press, 2000.

Heil, John. "Reader-Response and the Narrative Context of the Parables about Growing Seed in Mark 4:1–34," *Catholic Biblical Quarterly* 54.2 (1992) 271–286.

Resources for Further Study

Herzog, William R. *Parables as Subversive Speech: Jesus as Pedagogue of the Oppressed.* Louisville: Westminster/John Knox Press, 1994.

———. "Sowing Discord: The Parable of the Sower (Mark 4:1-9)," *Review and Expositor* 109.2 (2012) 187-198.

Hultgren, Arland J. *The Parables of Jesus: A Commentary.* Grand Rapids, MI: Eerdmans, 2000.

Hunter, A.M. (Archibald Macbride). *The Parables: Then and Now.* London: SCM Press, 1971.

Jeremias, Joachim. *The Parables of Jesus.* Translated by S.H. Hooke. New York, NY: Charles Scribner's Sons, 1955.

Jiménez, Pablo. "The Laborers of the Vineyard (Matthew 20:1-16): A Hispanic Homiletical Reading," *Journal for Preachers* 21.1 (1997) 35-40.

Kim, Yung Suk. *Jesus's Truth: Parables in Life.* Eugene, OR: Resource, 2018.

Knight, George. "Luke 16:19-31: The Rich Man and Lazarus." *Review and Expositor* 94.2 (1997) 277-283.

LaHurd, Carol. "Re-viewing Luke 15 with Arab Christian Women." In *A Feminist Companion to Luke*, edited by Amy-Jill Levine, 246-268. New York: Sheffield Academic, 2002.

Landry, David, and Ben May. "Honor Restored: New Light on the Parable of the Prudent Steward (Luke 16:1-8a)." *JBL* 119.2 (2000) 287-309.

Levine, Amy-Jill. *Short Stories by Jesus: The Enigmatic Parables of a Controversial Rabbi.* New York, NY: HarperOne, 2014.

McArthur, Harvey K. "The Parable of the Mustard Seed." *CBQ* 33 (1971) 198-201.

McIver, Robert K. "The parable of the weeds among the wheat (Matt 13:24-30, 36-43) and the relationship between the kingdom and the church as portrayed in the Gospel of Matthew." *JBL* 114.4 (1995) 643-659.

Meier, John. "The Parable of the Wheat and the Weeds (Matthew 13:24-30): Is Thomas's Version (Logion 57) Independent?" *JBL* 131.4 (2012) 715-732.

Park, Rohun. "Revisiting the parable of the prodigal son for decolonization: Luke's reconfiguration of *oikos* in Luke 15:11-32." *Biblical Interpretation* 17 (2009) 507-520.

Parsons, Mikeal. "The Prodigal's Older Brother: The History and Ethics of Reading Luke 15:25- 32." *Perspectives in Religious Studies* 23 (1996) 147-174.

Payne, Philip. "Order of Sowing and Ploughing in the Parable of the Sower." *NTS* 25.1 (1978) 123-29.

Perrin, Norman. *Rediscovering the Teaching of Jesus.* New York: Harper & Row, 1967.

Peterson, William L. "The Parable of the Lost Sheep in the Gospel of Thomas and the Synoptics." *Novum Testamentum* 23.2 (1981) 128-47.

Reid, Barbara. *Parables for Preachers,* Year A. Matthew. Collegeville, MN: Liturgical, 2001.

———. Year B. Mark. 1999.

———. Year C. Luke. 2000.

Resources for Further Study

Räisänen, Heikki. "The Prodigal Gentile and His Jewish Christian Brother, Luke 15:11-32." In *The Four Gospels*, edited by F. Van Segbroek *et al.*, 1617-36. Leuven: Leuven University Press, 1992.

Matthew S. Rindge. "Luke's Artistic Parables: Narratives of Subversion, Imagination, and Transformation," *Interpretation* 68 (2014) 403-415.

Rohrbaugh, Richard L. "A Peasant Reading of the Parable of the Talents/Pounds: A Text of Terror?" *BTB* 23.1 (1993) 32-39.

Schellenberg, Ryan. "Kingdom as Contaminant? The Role of Repertoire in the Parables of the Mustard Seed and the Leaven." *CBQ* 71.3 (2009) 527-543.

Schottroff, Luise. *The Parables of Jesus*. Minneapolis: Fortress, 2006.

Scott, Bernard. "Lost Junk, Found Treasure," *TBT* 26 (1988) 31-34.

―――. "The King's accounting: Matthew 18:23-34." *JBL* 104.3 (1985) 429-442.

―――. *Hear Then the Parable: A Commentary on the Parables of Jesus*. Minneapolis: Fortress Press, 1989.

―――. *Re-Imagine the World: An Introduction to the Parables of Jesus*. Santa Rosa, Calif.: Polebridge Press, 2001.

Snodgrass, Klyne R. *Stories with Intent: A Comprehensive Guide to the Parables of Jesus*. Grand Rapids, MI: Eerdmans, 2008.

Tevel, J. M. "The Laborers in the Vineyard: the Exegesis of Matthew 20:1-7 in the Early Church," *Vigiliae Christianae* 46 (1992) 356-380.

Ukpong, Justin. "The Parable of the Talents (Matt 25:14-30): Commendation or Critique of Exploitation?: A Social-Historical and Theological Reading." *Neotestamenica* 46.1 (2012) 190-207.

Waller, Elizabeth. "The parable of the leaven: a sectarian teaching and the inclusion of women," *Union Seminary Quarterly Review* 35.1-2 (1979-80) 99-109.

Westermann, Claus. *The Parables of Jesus in the Light of the Old Testament*. Minneapolis, MN: Fortress, 1990.

Wilder, Amos. *Early Christian Rhetoric: The Language of the Gospel*. Eugene, OR: Wipf & Stock, 2014.

―――. "The Parable of the Sower: Naïvete and Method in Interpretation." *Semeia* 2 (1974) 134-51.

Young, Brad. *The Parables: Jewish Tradition and Christian Interpretation*. Peabody, MA: Hendrickson Publishers, 1998.

www.ingramcontent.com/pod-product-compliance
Lightning Source LLC
Chambersburg PA
CBHW051705090426
42736CB00013B/2547